Cue Tips

Stage Management Handbook for High School Theatre

by

Elizabeth D. Ward

Petals & Pages
860 Polaris Blvd SE
Rio Rancho, NM 87124
petals_pages@msn.com

Published by Petals & Pages
Copyright 2006
ISBN 978-0-9797057-2-4

Special thanks to:

Harry McEnerny
and
Maury Hancock

Introduction

Stage management is probably the most difficult role in theatre to define due to the wide range of responsibilities that it encompasses. This hand book was created to familiarize you with those responsibilities as well as introduce methods and mindsets that will benefit you no matter what position you hold in theatre.

Designed specifically for high school students, this book takes into account relationships with peers, student/teacher relationships and academic responsibilities. You will find there are certain advantages to learning stage management while cast and crew are all in a central location. This book should help you enter into the role of stage manager during these early years of theatre training.

Although the specifics of the position vary from show to show, as well as venue to venue, the fundamental concepts and requirements are offered here. A stage manager's job begins before the auditions and is not over with the final blackout of closing night. The sooner you become accustomed to the process the better your stage management career will be.

In the first section, On the Art of Stage Management, you will find an emphasis on the qualities and attributes of leadership that you may already be developing as a student, but this text applies them to the stage manager's role. As a stage manager you will need to be aware of everything around you at all times. You must be able to solve problems quickly and effectively. You must motivate and encourage others, even when you are tired or discouraged. As a stage manager you need to be able to multi-task, prioritize and keep track of all kinds of information. To be a good stage manager you must have patience and you must take pride in what you do. The ability to judge situations and act in the best interests of the production is also critical. You must be able to communicate with many types of people and earn respect from them. And finally, as a stage manager you will need to understand the visions of others as well as learn to develop your own. These skills and qualities are all covered in this section.

The main body of this handbook deals with the production process, beginning with what happens when you first commit to a job. You will read about the stage manager / director relationship, how to best serve your director, what is expected of you and what you should expect from the director. From this first step this text will give you information on preparing a prompt book and a check list of tools and supplies that you should begin to acquire.

The audition is the next topic. In this section you will read about how to prepare for a group audition, including how to set up the space. There are also suggestions on running the audition and what needs to be done afterwards. Also included is information on scheduling, creating a callboard, finding a space and safety issues.

Rehearsals are where stage managers spend most of their time, and subsequently, it is during the rehearsal weeks that they do the most wide-ranging work. In this section you wil read about how to run rehearsals, spike furniture, deal with props and costumes, and how to run warm-ups. "Speed thrus" and "French scenes" are defined and you will find basic blocking methods and examples. Also explained is the importance of rehearsal reports and what should be included in them, prompting methods and the significance of timing conclude this section.

The next section deals with the stage manager's responsibilities beyond rehearsals. Production meetings are the most critical among them, although the others should not be ignored. You will find a description of what happens during these meetings and your role as the stage manager within them. The other duties discussed here are props assistance, shop visits and reflection on the project.

The Tech and Dress section that follows briefly describes the different technical and dress rehearsals that take place before performance week. Beginning with paper-tech, you will find information on how to notate cues in the script. The text goes on to prepare you for technical and dress rehearsals, explaining the purpose of each and offering suggestions on how to manage them.

The second to last section in this handbook is on performance. It contains a checklist of pre-show, performance and post show duties as well as headset/cue calling etiquette and procedures. You will also find information on how to refine your performance and make performance reports. No process would be complete without a strike, so logically, its significance is mentioned at the end of this section.

This handbook concludes with a section on evaluations and preservation. It was written with the intention to challenge you to examine your experience with a critical eye and to recognize the significance of documenting and preserving that experience.

This text will be most valuable to you in high school, will prepare you for college theatre and could even be of value to you in community theatre experiences. If you are interested in a professional career in stage management I suggest Thomas A. Kelly's The Backstage

Guide to Stage Management (1999), and Lawrence Stern's Stage Management (1998). Both of these resources are very thorough in detailing the stage manager's role in professional theatre and the rules of Actors' Equity Association are heavily emphasized.

Use this book as a guide in conjunction with your director. You may find that some things do not apply to your specific situation or that your director wants to withhold certain responsibilities. Proper communication will prevent misunderstandings and help you further define your position with each production.

An attempt was made to personalize the information in such a way that it will lead you to look beyond the facts and discover ways of adapting this information to your situation. The goal throughout the book is to alleviate some of the fears that you might have about the job and reinforce the idea that this is a learning experience. No one is flawless, especially when dealing with as many factors as a stage manager must.

·Part 1
The Art of Stage Management

Part 1
The Art of Stage Management

There is an art to stage management, although it's not one widely recognized or appreciated. Throughout history theatre productions have relied on the varied talents of stage managers and yet most people don't even know what they are, or what they do. As theatre innovations and procedures have become more complex over the years, the duties and definitions of stage managers have likewise become more expansive. No longer just prompters, stage managers have a wide range of responsibilities.

The stage manager is the communications link between members of the production team, a storehouse for the documentation of almost every element of a production; responsible for the schedule and maintenance of actors, and for overseeing the accomplishment of tasks required to mount, run and close a production. This sums up the duties of a stage manager, but there is far more involved with the job.

Responsibility is a key word when discussing stage management. By accepting a stage management position you agree to be held accountable for the outcome of important choices you make that ultimately effect the production. Not only are you responsible for your own actions but also the actions of others. For example, if you have a backstage crew that is unsure of their duties and something goes wrong during a performance because of this, you are responsible, even if you were sitting in the booth when it happened. It was your job to see that the crew understood what was supposed to happen.

The weight of responsibility tends to bear heavily on the mind at times. I know people who claim that they stage-managed once and could never do it again because the job was too hard, too time consuming, too stressful. One said she still has nightmares about the experience. I have to admit, nightmares do sometimes come with the job, but this is no reason to be afraid of doing something that can give so much satisfaction.

In order to be a responsible stage manager it is important to develop and improve upon the following qualities and skills that are critical in any leadership position. These don't all come easily, at least not to everyone, and you should not be discouraged if you fail at times. I should say, *when* you fail. Mistakes *will* happen. If it weren't for the mistakes we would never learn to improve or succeed at what we do.

Ten Stage Management Skills & Qualities

Awareness

A major component of responsibility is awareness (Faust 4). As a stage manager it is important that you know as much as possible about everything.

Environment
You cannot do your job effectively if you are unfamiliar with the working environment. I suggest that you walk through the theatre every day. Just look around and see what is

there. Examine the stage and backstage areas carefully. Notice what is different from one day to the next. Who else uses the space and for what purpose? Do you see any dangers? How much light does the back door let in? If you had to walk through in total darkness what would you be concerned about? What sounds does the theatre make? Do pipes clank when the heat comes on? Can you hear people in rooms above or next to the theatre?

Where is the fire extinguisher? First aid? Every theatre has its own peculiarities. The more you know about them the fewer surprises there will be.

Situations

I can't possibly predict every situation that you will find yourself in. I can tell you, though; the best way to deal with them is to know as much as you can. If an actor is late, before you threaten to throw him off the roof, know the facts. Before you decide on make-up calls, find out people's schedules.

In rehearsals be fully aware of who is doing what on stage, off stage and backstage if possible. I don't just mean what people involved in the scene are doing, but even those cast members who aren't in the scene being worked. For one thing, you want to make certain they are behaving. Get to know their habits when they wait in the wings. Observing such details, big or small, can save a performance. If, for example, during the last few full run rehearsals, two of your supporting male actors had the habit of visiting the lead female in the downstage left wing and their next entrance is stage right, make a mental note of that. Come opening night, when your assistant stage manager (ASM) who is working to get the actors in position, says that those two actors aren't where they are supposed to be, you can tell her where to find them.

Another benefit from these observations is that it gives you the ability to improvise. Consider this situation: There is a costume quick change two pages away. There are four actors involved and all of your wardrobe crew is assigned to help, however, one of the crew is feeling ill. She is out back and around the corner trying to get some fresh air and loses track of time. Your ASM discovers the crew member missing and tells you. You have cues coming up and you know that your ASM has duties that prevent her from helping with the change. What do you do? You happen to know that there is a particular cast member who, very responsibly stays backstage even though he doesn't go on for a long time yet. Have your ASM assign that actor to the costume change and another to locate the costumer and go on with the show. This could all have been avoided, however, if you were aware, before the show, that you had a crew member feeling ill. The whole cast and crew could have been on alert.

There is a great number of things to be aware of. Sometimes stage management requires eyes in the back of your head, supersonic hearing and telepathic capabilities. It takes a lot of practice to really develop these traits. You don't have to limit this practice to rehearsals. Always be aware of what's going on around you.

Personal

I wouldn't dare tell you that stage managers never get upset, frustrated or discouraged. We are human, after all. It's ok to have feelings. What is important is how we express them. In order to deal with our feelings effectively we need to understand where they are coming from.

Let's say you failed a French test, you missed lunch, lost your favorite pen, then your car broke down before rehearsal. You arrive a few minutes later than you wanted to, but not late. The cast shows up, they are a little more rowdy than usual. Are you going to get really mad and crack the whip? Or are you going to completely ignore them and spend most of rehearsal chewing on your pencil and wishing it was time to go? You aren't mad at the actors, and you can't solve anything by "spacing out" during rehearsal. You are going to take a deep breath, and with a hint of demanding, a touch of pleading, and a little love, you will ask them to behave. They will see that you are serious, and instead of being afraid of you they will want to please you by keeping themselves quiet.

Just because stage managers work backstage doesn't mean they aren't performers. You are performing every time you enter a theatre. Be aware of how others see you. How do you want them to see you? Do you gossip? Does your body language give away things you don't want known, such as confusion, anxiety or frustration? People put a lot of faith in stage managers; don't give them reason to doubt. It's a pretty tall order when you think about it. Don't stress over this, just be aware.

Problem solving skills

Problems will arise. The question is "How are you going to handle them?" Stephen E. Lucas, in his book, *The Art of Public Speaking* proposes the following five steps:

1.   Define the problem

2.   Analyze it. How does it affect the production? Who does it involve? Are there safety issues? Are there time constraints?

3.   Develop criteria for a solution. What needs to happen? What is the ultimate goal?

4.   Brainstorm. Come up with multiple options and calculate the outcomes.

5.   Select the solution. Find the most suitable solution and implement it.

Remember that you don't have to do all this on your own. You are a leader and part of leadership is working with others.

Troubleshooting will help you solve some production problems before they occur. We all know that what can go wrong will go wrong - if you don't anticipate it. Learn to ask yourself a series of "what if's" that are relevant to the show. For example:
What if the Zippo Lighter doesn't work to light the candle in scene 2?
Solution: Fill with lighter fluid, check the flint before the show and have matches or a backup lighter near the candle.

You may come up with some ridiculous possibilities, but when one actually happens you will be prepared.

I once worked on a show called, *La Nona*, in which the lead actor was required to eat a ridiculous amount of food throughout the night, including pasta, chips, cookies and fruit. One night a bag of chips burst open and spilled all over the floor. When another performer discovered the mess, she took a small broom and dustpan from under the sink and cleaned it up, in character. The broom and dust pan were never used otherwise. Be certain to tell your performers about any backup emergency props you add to the set or your preparation is pointless.

Motivation

It is the responsibility of the stage manager to maintain the spirit of the cast and crew. There will be days when your cast comes in and no one is happy. This is no way to start a rehearsal. You may be just as unhappy, tired, or frustrated as they are, but you have to leave all personal worries and discomforts outside and set an example for others to follow. Your director wants to work with energetic, living beings. If you can't even live up to that then the director shouldn't bother coming to rehearsal. Remember, if you lose faith in a project the cast and crew loses faith. If your commitment is weak, their commitment will be weak.

Be nice to people. Don't gossip. Make them feel special, talented and appreciated. Everyone has different needs. Try to discover what they are. Those actors we call "Divas" for example, love to talk about themselves. Ask them questions that you know they want to answer. Compliment them. Jokers like to play, so let them make you smile. The flirts - deal with them as you see fit. The point is, the more you can give them what they need the happier they will be to give you what you need.

Organization

Organization isn't just about having a well assembled prompt book and carefully laid out props. It requires time management and detailed record keeping. As for making the most of your time, the best advice is to have a TO DO LIST and an HOURLY SCHEDULE. Schedule time to take care of the items on your list. Also, consider how much time you spend in the car on the way home, or waiting outside a classroom for a friend. When you can't actually DO something physically, THINK productively. You don't have to spend every free hour of your day working physically and mentally on a production, but do begin training yourself to think beyond rehearsal and learn to use time wisely.

Keeping good records is an often painstaking, yet vital part of the job. You will have so many pieces of information to keep track of. During rehearsals you need to accurately account for everything within the show. Rehearsal report, prop lists, etc. will help you maintain that information. When you are not in rehearsal you will come across things, such as phone numbers, important dates and questions that people need for you to find the answers to. Write down everything, don't try to remember it. Date everything, every question and phone conversation. Star critical or high priority information. When you complete a task, find the answer to a question, etc. mark it off with a big check mark so that you know with a glance that it is done.

Don't throw away anything. Keep a shoebox to store papers, envelopes you have written notes on, the pop quiz you created a list of questions on the back of, Post-It notes, etc., even if you have transferred the information from paper scraps to your prompt book, save those scraps. By saving all this information you won't spend time digging through your trash for something that you discover you need again.

People will rely on you to have accurate information about the show. Actors will ask you where they are supposed to be on stage, a light operator will expect you to know when lights come in and out, members of the audience expect to be entertained without the distractions of faulty cues and disorganized scene changes. Keep track of everything and make certain that your prompt script is clearly understandable, in case someone needs to take over for you in an emergency.

Patience

Patience truly is a virtue. A stage manager who lacks patience will never survive. We deal with so many factors, and so many people. Without patience how could we hope to listen to others we disagree with and understand their opinions? How can we remain calm when chaos breaks out?

You will find yourself in many situations where the easiest thing to do would be to throw your book on the table, growl something under your breath and storm out of the building. During "tech" for example, when the hours have been long and your actors are exhausted, your director is frustrated, your assistant stage manager is confused and you have an inexperienced board operator and they are all hounding you, you have to take a deep breath and remain calm.

In general, you should possess an easy, calm temperament. Be approachable. When things start to get unstable it won't take much to show your actors that you are serious, and they will be more accommodating. If you are generally unapproachable or irritable, or turn nasty when things get rough, then people will take great pleasure in annoying you.

Judgement

There are many variables that effect the decisions you will have to make. The more information you have the better off you will be. This is where your "awareness" is going to really pay off. You will have to make decisions based on knowledge of the show, the situation, the people involved, the mood, the time frame, etc. What is most beneficial for the production?

Here are some potential situations to consider as examples. A fit of laughter amongst director and cast. Is it a misuse of time or is it in some way therapeutic and good for the sense of ensemble or bonding? Should you stop it or let them get it out of their system? Learn when to share in the moment and when to crack the whip, and how to do them both at the same time.

A light cue was missed and action on stage keeps going. How important is the cue? Do you make the audience aware of the mistake by fading it in, or is the scene better off the way the way it is?

Sometimes it's best to leave things the way they are, but other times you must do something. A stagehand fails to secure one of two huge rolling step units during the stage change. In 45 seconds 30 singers and dancers will reach the stage from the aisles of the house and the lights are full on stage. Do you send someone on stage to correct the mistake or do you pray that the fifteen actors about to climb the unit don't die? You send a stage hand on, in front of 300 people and say, "Don't come back until you know it is bolted." The more you understand the show, the director, etc., the better your judgement will be.

Communication skills

Being able to communicate effectively will be one of your greatest assets. The stage manager has all the facts, or at least knows where to find them. People will come to you for critical information and you have to be able to express yourself clearly and concisely. Every day, people will be counting on your instruction, and if you sound like you don't know what you are talking about, then they will stop listening to you. When unsure of something, don't make hasty decisions or give false information. Just assure them that you will find out what they need to know and get back to them.

Sometimes communication is in the form of notes on the callboard, phone or email messages. Whatever form it takes, make certain that information is both received and understood. When speaking with someone, think before you speak. Know what you need to say. Listen closely when others speak to you. Try not to make people repeat themselves, especially your director. If you aren't certain about something said you must clarify it, so listen close the first time. Look people in the eye, so that they know you are paying attention.

Developing relationships with cast and crew is also critical. Be able to talk to anyone. As I mentioned earlier, you have to be able to understand the opinions and needs of others.

Respect

The Golden Rule, *Do unto others as you would have done unto you,* is a good first step in gaining respect. What is it that you want? Recognition? Appreciation? A hug? Be honest and sincere with everyone. Listen, encourage and appreciate. Respect them and they will respect you.

The second step is empowerment, being able to take control. Stage managers hold a high position of authority. In a high school situation there are adults who have the ultimate authority, but with any luck will only exercise that control in instances that are beyond your experience. Aside from those times it is the stage manager who is in charge and you will most likely find yourself telling adults what to do. For example, if there is a teacher in the cast they should be expected to follow your lead. Even the technical director will look to you to make certain decisions or pass on instruction.

You cannot be intimidated by older or more experienced people. You have an important job and you need to have confidence to exert authority. When control is taken over or a decision is made that you feel you should have a say in, don't get upset. It is understandable that you feel frustrated by this, but you will have to accept it without making a scene.

You may have lost control briefly over a situation, but don't lose control over your emotions, especially not in front of those who expect to see your strength. Remember, it is possible to be in control without being abusive. No one wants to work for a tyrant.

When you do something wrong, or fail to do something, be the first to recognize and admit it. Acknowledge your mistakes; don't try to hide from them. It shows strength of character. Remember, there are many ways to apologize or accept responsibility for things without using the words "I'm sorry." You may not understand now, but if you aren't careful those two words will ring in your ears and slowly destroy your confidence. You will begin to feel sorry, in all forms of the word, and after that it's hard to respect yourself.

17

Another challenge that you might face is having authority over your peers. You have to be as diplomatic as possible. Don't favor particular people and ignore or mistreat others. Treat them all equally. The more they see that you are not the enemy, the more willing they will be to please you. Be careful, if they don't take you seriously they will take advantage of you. Once you have lost control it's hard, if not impossible, to get it back.

Vision

Everyone who works on a show has a vision. The director has one, the designers have one, even the actors have a vision. When a director chooses a script she or he will develop an interpretation of that script. By emphasizing specific themes and emotions and supporting them with design concepts, a vision is created. There is more to it but that should give you the idea. The director works closely with the designers and actors to further develop the vision. A stage manager needs to be in tune with these visions in order to help them become a reality.

Understand what your director wants and keep an eye on the goal throughout the process. Listen closely and get a feel for how the director works with and develops scenes. Recognize the director's methods for motivating and inspiring the actors. What outcomes please or displease the director? If you were stage managing a professional show with a long run, it is likely that the director would leave you responsible for maintaining it ater opening night. The longer a show runs, the more it evolves, and not always for the better. When things veer off course you will need to restore the show to the director's original vision. Make certain you know what that vision is.

Stage managers need vision as much as anyone: vision for overall concepts as well as details of design and directional choices. Develop an eye for stage pictures, strength within actor's choices, see what works and what doesn't. Consider the idea of acoustical vision. Listen to the tones, the rhythms, the levels of voices, entire scenes and the play as a whole. If you're lucky you will have a director who is interested in your opinion and will listen to your ideas.

Pride

It's easy to become overwhelmed by the job, lose faith in yourself, and take things personally, but confidence is critical. Even if you aren't exactly sure of everything, you have to feel confident that things are going to work out. Take pride in the knowledge that you can calm nerves, find lost items, and diffuse arguments. When you call a complicated sequence of cues, have a successful show, or avoid panicking where there is a problem you should feel great about yourself. When you begin to feel unsure remember what you have accomplished in the past and have faith in your abilities. If you give it all you've got and challenge yourself, that also is something to be proud of.

So why would anyone want to be a stage manager when it involves all this responsibility?

There are many reasons:

☞ The brief but intense time spent with so many diverse people.

☞ Witnessing the creation and evolution of a production.

☞ Being a part of the process and ultimately "calling the shots."

☞ To challenge yourself.

☞ To be awed by actors in their moments of glory when a week before they couldn't even get their lines right.

Stage managers don't win awards, and they don't get publicity. What they do get is the respect of their cast and crew, and other company members, a boost in confidence, personal satisfaction and a sense of accomplishment.

Stage management is a critical part of production and, even though it's frustrating, someone has to do it. If you can accomplish the basics set forth in this book you should have little trouble being successful as a stage manager.

Part 2
The Process

Part 2
The Process
Pre-Auditions

Getting the Job
Some jobs you will have to search for, others will fall into your lap. Regardless of whether you are in school or an equity stage manager in New York, from the first moment you commit, you should focus on the project. Do everything you can to prepare. Create, or replenish, your *Stage Manager's box*. Check your calendar for potential schedule conflicts. Prepare yourself mentally for what is to come.

Expectations
Meet with the director as soon as possible to discuss what her or his expectations are concerning you. Every director has his or her own idea of what a stage manager does and how to work with one. Having this early discussion will prevent any misunderstandings. You may find that you have higher expectations for yourself than the director has for you. If there are duties that you are accustomed to doing, or you that you feel are necessary and the director doesn't mention them, let the director know. He or she may be glad to have someone who will go beyond expectations. Others may ask you not to go to the extra work.

Preparation of materials

1. Audition forms - Typically, the stage manager prepares a form to hand out at auditions. If you are given that responsibility in high school you will want to include space for the following information:

Name
Address
Phone, Cell phone, email
Special skills
Known schedule conflicts, and other potential conflicts
Show information, including show dates, if known

2. Sides/Play description - Every director will run auditions differently. Some will put together sides for cold readings and others will ask for prepared monologues. Whatever they do there will most likely be handout materials. Make certain that you get these, have plenty of copies made and put up any notices relevant to the location, date and time of the audition.

3. Stage management team - Part of being a leader is learning how to delegate. If you do have an assistant stage manager allow her or him to help you but do not abuse your assistant stage manager with either too much work or not enough. Perhaps you will leave her or him in charge of all props, or taking line notes. Have a discussion with your assistant and clearly define duties and expectations.

You may have a situation in which there are multiple stage managers for a production. For example, a theatre festival made up of seven one act plays may have three stage managers involved. During the rehearsal process these stage managers need to work together, share information with each other and plan things so that during a production they will all know what to expect. This situation would also require a production stage manager who is in charge of calling the show. The stage managers of the individual pieces would then split backstage duties, seeing to it that scenes shift smoothly, actors get in places and that props and costumes are all dealt with accordingly. There are a number of responsibilities that can be shared, the objective is to agree on things, work together to compromise and to strategize.

The Prompt Book

The prompt book is the official record for the production. You are responsible for seeing that all the necessary information gets into the prompt book and is kept up to date.

Start creating this with any information you have as soon as you are involved with the project. Add prompt script as soon as you get it.

Using dividers, create sections for:
The prompt script
Lights
Emergency information
Props
Preset sheets
Set
Scene breakdowns
Costumes
Requirement lists
Sound
Ground plans
Pronunciation guides
Rehearsal/production reports
Contact sheets
Schedules

In the prompt script you will keep track of everything that takes place during the performance. This includes all the actors blocking and all cues.

1. Make certain that there is plenty of space around the text with a blank page opposite it. Sometimes this requires cutting and pasting and photo copying. If you are right handed I would recommend that the blank page be on the right for all blocking and your text page be on the left where the cues will be added.

2. Using a series of index tabs, breakdown the script by acts and scenes. Each scene should start on its own page. Coordinate with your director on this aspect of organization.

3.   It is important that everything in the prompt book be well organized and clearly written.If, for some reason, you can't make it to a rehearsal or performance, then make certain someone else is available to take your place.

4.   There will be times when you will need to take the script home with you, but as much as possible during rehearsals, and always during performance week, leave the book at the theatre.

Script Research

When you first get the script, I would suggest that you read it right away. Put aside any preconceived notions of the script, including memories of past performances of the play that you may have seen.

Your initial reading should be for enjoyment. Familiarize yourself with the story. Then, read it again with a highlighter and mark all references to potential requirements (sound effects, props, etc.) that you find in the scene descriptions and within the dialogue. You may want to do several readings like this focusing on one technical aspect at a time. For example, highlight all prop references, read again and highlight all costumes, etc. With all the information highlighted in different colors you can begin making preliminary requirement lists. Discuss with your director which requirements will actually be used in the production.

Tools and Supplies

As stage manager you can expect the cast and crew to come to you for just about anything. You should begin to build a Stage Management (SM) Box that contains the following supplies that you will find useful. This does require a small investment, but creating it over time helps. Your school should also provide a good many of these materials. It isn't necessary to carry the tools with you, but you should have easy access to them. You don't want your box to get so heavy that you cannot carry it easily. If you leave it at the theatre, make certain that it is safely locked and stored.

Pharmaceutical
Ace bandage
Antacids
Antiseptic wipes
Aspirin
Bandaids
Burn cream
Cough drops
Tweezers
Permission slips may be required before giving any over the counter medications. Check your school policy manual.

Office supplies
Erasers
Glue, glue stick
Folders
Markers
Paper, blank
Pencils & pen
Ruler
Scissors
Stapler
Stop watch
Three hole punch, or paper punch

Tapes
Gaff tape
Glow tape
Masking tape
Scotch tape
Spike tape

Miscellaneous
Bobby pins
Breath mints
Candy, *Be aware of any students who are diabetic*
Extension cord
Nail clippers
Needles & Thread
Safety pins
Tampons, or individually wrapped sanitary napkins
Tissues

I suggest that you have a few small toys with you to entertain bored actors. A small Rubik's Cube, or something to keep their hands busy will help them to sit quietly instead of distracting others during rehearsal.

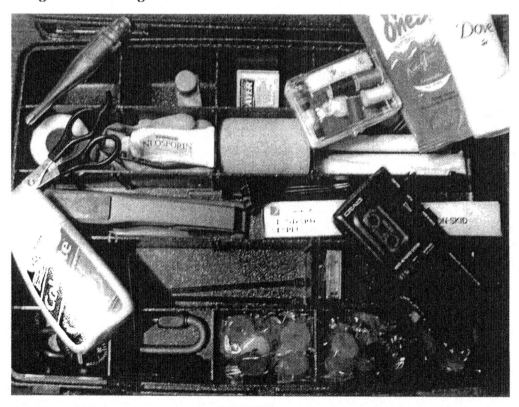

Auditions

Setting up the audition

High school auditions are usually group auditions that allow directors to judge not only a specific actor's talent but also how well different combinations of actors work together.

You will need to arrive early to prepare for the auditions. The first thing you should do is sweep the audition space. If the director wants everyone on stage as opposed to sitting in the house, then set up plenty of chairs in a circle. Provide a table for you, your assistant stage manager and the director on stage as well. Don't separate yourself from the situation by sitting at a table in the house. You want everyone to be aware of your presence and participation, right from the start.

All materials (audition forms, conflict schedules, show information, etc.) that will be needed should be set up and ready when actors arrive. If you want people to pick up this information themselves place these materials in neat stacks on the table and as people enter let them know where it is.

Running the Audition

Stage managers have as much responsibility during auditions as in rehearsal. One thing you need to do is collect everyone's audition forms and keep track of them throughout the process. Make note of what parts they read and who they read with. Consider noting anything substantial about their audition, such as; a strong voice, good chemistry with so and so, and anything that might help the director refresh her or his memory after the audition.

Large auditions can sometimes get difficult. You will need to arrange things so that everything runs as smoothly as possible, and that you keep your director on track. When there are only thirty minutes left according to the schedule, let the director know so that she or he can begin to wrap things up.

Audition Form

Production:_____Name_____

Class _____

Address _____

_____

Phone (____)____-_____Cell phone (____)____-_____

E-mail_____

Special Skills:

_____

_____

_____

Potential Conflicts: School, family, church, sports, scouts, etc.

_____

_____

_____

Be thorough -Once the schedule is set you will be expected to attend.

Schedule

Mark off times that you are in class or working. Be very clear. Rehearsals will be scheduled according to these forms. Some may be planned for mornings, afternoons and evenings.

Time	Mon	Tue	Wed	Thur	Fri	Sat	Sun
8:00							
9:00							
10:00							
11:00							
Noon							
1:00							
2:00							
3:00							
4:00							
5:00							
6:00							
7:00							
8:00							
9:00							
10:00							

After the audition

Following the auditions you will want to turn over all audition forms to the director. Depending on your director, you may or may not be involved in the decision process. Everything in regards to the audition process is confidential. You can't repeat what is discussed during the process, nor can you mention any notes the director makes about an actor on her or his audition form.

Once the director has given you the call-back list, post it on the callboard. The cast list is not official until it has been posted. Never tell someone they are cast before the list is up. When posting the cast list include a special "thank you" to everyone who auditioned. Also provide information about the time and date of the first rehearsal.

Contact Sheet
Once the show has been cast, using the information collected from the audition form, you will need to create a contact sheet. Provide phone numbers, cell phone numbers and email addresses, character name or position for the actors, director, stage managers and any crew members that you know are working on the show. This can be a digital file.

Schedules
Chances are you won't be responsible for creating a rehearsal schedule, however, I strongly recommend that you take part in the process. Be aware of campus activities and know what conflicts people have so that when the director decides to spontaneously add or alter a rehearsal, you will know whether or not it is possible.

Scheduling can be a grueling process. If you continue stage managing beyond high school you will have to do it. Scene breakdowns and conflict schedules will make the job easier.

Callboards
As the information hub, callboards are essential. This is where you will post everything, including copies of the rehearsal schedule, announcements and any notes that you have for the actors. Provide space for each department to receive daily rehearsal reports, and space for stage managers to receive their notes.

The callboard is for important information. It should not be used primarily for production members to leave personal, non-show related messages for each other.

All postings should be dated, and you should encourage everyone to check the board as often as possible. One way to make certain that they keep checking is to see that something is left for everyone at least once a week. This will also make everyone feel included.

Space

At some point you may find that the theatre is unavailable for rehearsal and you need to find an alternate space. The art room and lower school assembly hall are good options. The important thing to look for is a place is large enough to approximate the stage. The room should be clean, have places to sit and have phone access.

If your alternate location is a borrowed space you will have to take extra measures to ensure that it is kept up properly. Make certain that anything the cast brings into the room is removed at the end of the rehearsal. If furniture is used, return it to its original position. Always leave a room the way you found it.

Safety

Throughout the rehearsal and production process it is important to maintain a safe working environment. Be aware of any hazzards within the theatre and all emergency procedures associated with the space. Find out where all fire extinguishers are located and learn how to use them.

Accidents happen and you need to be prepared with first aide materials and the number of the campus nurse, nearest urgent care and other emergency numbers.

Any potentially dangerous physical requirements within a production, especially stage combat should be very closely supervised. Take things slowly at first, then, as actors become more comfortable, allow them to increase the pace.

Safety notes

- Props should only be handled by the specific actors who use them, the props crew and the stage management crew.

- Shoes must be worn at all times. If an actor must go barefoot for production, make certain they have shoes off stage.

- Always check stage and backstage for hazzards such as screws or nails sticking out of boards, tools left out, low hanging cords, etc.

- Always check stability of flats, platforms, rigged items, etc.

- Know how the set was built, how special items work (i.e. waterfalls, revolves) and how objects were hung.

- Don't allow horseplay on set.

- Walk through sets, especially multi-level ones to make certain railings, step units, etc. are safe. This will ease your actors' fears about the set.

- Make certain that warm-ups are done before any physical strenuous actions are rehearsed or performed.

- If someone isn't feeling well, let him or her sit down or go home. You don't want to wear them out or infect the cast.

- During production, bring in fruit and bottled water, not junk food, for your actors.

Rehearsals

The majority of stage manager's duties take place in rehearsal. Something new happens every rehearsal and it is critical that you attend each one. I understand that in high school there are certain factors that can prevent you from being there. For example, if you are sick and don't go to classes, you cannot do after school activities. In college and professional theatre, calling in sick or without transportation is not an option. In fact, stage managers do whatever they have to in order to be at rehearsal because they know that even one day of missed information could prove to be a problem in the long run. Do your best to stay healthy and be smart about making other commitments. In the event you must miss rehearsal an assistant stage manager will be of great benefit.

The First Rehearsal

The first rehearsal is very important because first impressions are lasting ones, so you will want to be full of energy and confidence. At the start of the rehearsal tell the cast who you are, why you are there and how much you look forward to working with everyone. Let them know what they can expect from you. For example, they can expect to see you working as hard as they do and putting the same time commitment. They can expect you to know what is going on during rehearsal and performances, and that you will keep things running smoothly. They can expect you to be there for them for anything from a break up to a broken nail. Ask them to tell you when you are failing in this.

Let them know what you expect of them, including:

Patience in rehearsals
No gum in rehearsal
No playing with props
Always have a pencil
Bring homework to do
Bring your script
Check the callboard
Always let SM know if you leave the rehearsal area
Always check with SM before leaving for the day

Once you are done with your announcements, answer any questions the cast has for you and then turn things back over to the director.

The director will probably take the time during the first rehearsal to discuss his or her vision for the show, at least certain aspects of it. They might mention why they have chosen the script and what they hope to do with the characters staging. This is good information to note.

Following the director's talk with the cast you will want to start the reading of the scipt. Having everyone seated in a circle is the best set-up. The read will probably go slowly because the actors are unfamiliar with their lines and may not have marked off their roles for easy reference. Time this read anyway.

During the read the director may give cuts or alterations. Mark these clearly in pencil. Before everyone leaves make certain that they are clear about the schedule and that there are no major conflicts.

Setting up

Consistency is very important in all areas of stage management for several reasons. One is that it keeps you on track. Another reason is, just as you are aware of the actors' habits, they become aware of yours. They will come to depend on them! The best advice when it comes to setting things up, is to have a routine.

35

Included in your routine should be the following:

1. Always be early

2. Clear the stage of anything you can, that isn't used in the show

3. Sweep the stage thoroughly - not into the wings.

4. Set the furniture and props according to the schedule.

Spiking

As soon as you have a good idea where furniture will be placed on stage you should spike it using colored spike tape. Mark the upstage floor corners or legs of the piece. If necessary use a marker to label it. Throughout rehearsals the tape will loosen. It helps to cover the spike take with scotch tape. Keep an eye on it and replace tape before it gets bad. If any furniture moves during scene changes make certain that they are clearly visible for your shift crew. Re-tape the necessary spikes after the floor has been painted for the production.

> **Note: Meet with your technical director as soon as possible and mark the layout of the set on the floor with spike tape.**

Props

Ask your props master to get you rehearsal props as soon as possible. The sooner they get props into their hands the sooner they will get rid of their script. They also need to become familiar with where props come from and where they go during the course of the show.

Begin with critical props. Props that help define a character, like a pipe or a cane. As actors get off book you will want to have as many rehearsal props as possible. If your props master cannot come up with the actual item, request blocks of wood that can represent the prop. Using a marker, label each one.

Space should be provided for props offstage where actors can easily access them. Tape off a table providing a spot for each prop and label each. Write the item, act and scene number clearly. You may not have enough room back stage during the rehearsal process for a table full of props. Find something, perhaps a trunk or a bookshelf, and make certain the actors know exactly where to pick up and return their props.

There are some props that need to be stored more securely than most; things such as weapons, cigarettes, lighters and expensive items. Only a few people should have access to these. They should be locked up and only retrieved when they are needed for rehearsal or performance.

Furniture

It is important for actors during the blocking period to understand the dimensions and movement patterns in which they will be performing. In those early weeks of rehearsal you may have to improvise when it comes to furniture and set pieces. Locate what you can to substitute for missing pieces and do your best to approximate the final set.

Costumes

Costumes aren't generally needed during the rehearsal process unless they are critical to the development of a character or it is critical for an actor to become accustomed to them. For example, an actor who will be wearing high heels will need to get used to the shoes well before production. Or, let's say a long cloak is worn that truly needs to become an extension of the actor, so much a part of him that he instinctively uses it to enhance the character. Such costumes as these and the ones that are used as props should be incorporated into the rehearsal process as soon as possible.

Running Rehearsal

One of the most important things you need to do in rehearsals is to pay close attention to the director, even if she or he is working one-on-one with an actor. Anticipate what your director needs at any given time and try to assist. Whether it means silencing the cast, or bringing the director the script that was left on stage, try to accomplish these things before they are forced to ask. You will also need to keep your director informed on the status, such as letting him or her know that all actors are present except one, whom you have called and is, or isn't, on the way. Also keep the director aware when 30 minutes and 5 minutes are left of rehearsal time. If you can keep your director from going overtime, your actors will love you.

Maintaining a productive work environment is another duty of the stage manager. This means eliminating distractions like chatty visitors, preserving your work space by keeping it clean and clutter free, and being aware of safety hazzards and taking precautions.

When it comes to noise, every director has a different tolerance for it. It will not take you long to discover her or his breaking point if you ignore the actors conversing I the corner of the room behind you. It all depends on the situation. If you have five people in rehearsal and the director is working with three and the other two are being halfway productive in the back of the room, just keep them at a reasonable volume. When you have a cast of twelve, and they all have to stay in the theatre, chances are you will have to quiet them repeatedly. Start with a polite "sshhh!" If that doesn't work, a firm "Quiet in the house, please" is the next step. If the problem persists, single out the trouble makers, eventually your director will no doubt step in, and at least he or she will know that you tried.

Don't forget to set a good example yourself. This means no idle chatting with friends when the director is working a scene.

Warm-Ups

Actors in college and professional theatre come to rehearsals ready to work. They tend to jump right into their own warm-ups and focusing techniques. In high school you will find that your actors want to talk to their friends. Encourage those that come early, and everyone else as they enter, to begin focusing. When it's time for rehearsal to begin, you should call everyone into a warm-up circle. Don't make your director do this. If the director is running late you can begin the warm-ups. Your director will be pleased to see everyone working when she or he arrives.

You have two options when it comes to starting warm-ups without your director. Your first option is to ask for a volunteer from the cast to take over, or you can do it yourself. Whenever possible have a cast member lead them. You should be familiar with the vocal and physical warm-ups that your director uses so that you can do the same.

> **Note: whenever possible join the cast in doing warm-ups.**

"Speed Thrus"

Some directors have their cast read through or run the lines of a scene or act before working them. Each rehearsal this is done the process should become faster. There are at least two benefits from this process.

The first benefit is that it helps actors learn their lines. Sometimes, when dealing with actions and character, actors will paraphrase the script. They begin to repeat their mistakes when they are off book. These read/speed thrus will keep them focused on the lines and increase accuracy. As actors become more and more familiar with their lines the speed will increase.

The second benefit is that it helps the actors develop a rhythm for their character, and for the show as a whole. For productions that depend on perfect comic timing and a fast pace this process will be an invaluable tool for the director.

"French" Scenes

"French" scenes are scenes in which the number of characters on stage remains the same. Within one scripted scene there can be many French scenes. Any time an actor enters or exits a new French scene begins. Draw diagrams of actor's positions at the end of each French scene. When a director wants to start from a particular entrance, you will know where everyone needs to be.

Blocking

One of the director's jobs is to tell actors where to go and what to do. These instructions are called "blocking." All traffic patterns and activities made by actors are blocked and must be notated on the prompt script (note: make certain that all actors are also recording all of their blocking). Blocking can, and will, change periodically and should be written clearly in pencil only.

Every stage manager tends to note blocking differently. Some prefer shorthand, some long, or a combination. If you use any symbols or short hand notation then you should include a blocking key in your prompt script that describes them.

Example of blocking notation
Chris returns to stage right chair and sits before Alex enters.
C   rtrns → sr.ch :s b4   A   ent.___

Stage Locations

Small stage

UR	UC	UL
R	C	L
DR	DC	DL

Large stage

UR	URC	UC	ULC	UL
R	RC	C	LC	L
DR	DRC	DC	DLC	DL

Sample Blocking Key

L - Left	U - Up stage	↑ - up stage (of)	ch - chair	
R - Right	D - Down stage	↓ - down stage (of)	st - step	
C - Center	G - give	∞ - turns		
S - sit	F - face	→ - to	hnd - hand	
S - stand	" - speaks(or says)	⊤ - table	ft - foot	
X - cross	ent - enter	xt - exit	p/u - pick up	
Rtrns – returns	xcpt – except	b4 - before	aft - after	

Example of notation from script for *As You Like It*

78   AS YOU LIKE IT   [ACT III

Ros. But are you so much in love as your rhymes speak?

Orl. Neither rhyme nor reason can express how much.

Ros. Love is merely a madness, and I tell you, deserves
as well a dark house and a whip as madmen do;
and the reason why they are not so punished and
cured is that the lunacy is so ordinary that the
whippers are in love too. Yet I profess curing it by
counsel.

Orl. Did you ever cure any so?

Ros. Yes, one, and in this manner. He was to imagine
me his love, his mistress; and I set him every day
to woo me. At which time would I, being but a
moonish youth, grieve, be effeminate, changeable,
longing and liking, proud, fantastical, apish,
shallow, inconstant, full of tears, full of smiles, for
every passion something and for no passion truly
anything, as boys and women are for the most part
cattle of this colour; would now like him, now
loathe him; then entertain him, then forswear
him; now weep for him, then spit at him; that I
drave my suitor from his mad humour of love to a
living humour of madness, which was, to forswear
the full stream of the world and to live in a nook
merely monastic. And thus I cured him, and this
way will I take upon me to wash your liver as clean
as a sound sheep's heart, that there shall not be one
spot of love in't.

Orl. I would not be cured, youth.

Ros. I would cure you, if you would but call me Rosa-

Schneider Notation System

A woman named Doris Schneider, an experienced stage manager and teacher, among other things, has written a book, The Art and Craft of Stage Management (1997). It was a book designed for students in the college/university setting. In this book is a highly developed and efficient notation system that I recommend to any student stage manager.

Rehearsal Reports

Daily rehearsal reports are required for every university and professional production. Get into the habit of making them now. They are a way to let everyone know what is going on, what the production needs. Keep them in order in your prompt script.

Information should include the following:

Name of show
Director
Stage Manager
Date
Location
Start, stop and break times
Attendance: who is present and who is missing? Any special guests?
Activities: record time spent on warm-ups, read thrus, scene work (always note what scenes are worked)
Props: you should note what props you don't have, props that need to be fixed, any questions about props, etc. Anything related to props should go here. Continue to note every day until you get the props, get them fixed, or get questions answered.
Set: is there a set piece missing, broken, too big? Are tools being left on the stage?
Sound & lights: any time you hear the director mention what will happen, or what he or she would like to have happen with sound or lights, write it down. Write down any questions that occur concerning sound and lights.
Costumes: same as above.
Miscellaneous: Announcements, problems, concerns and questions

These reports need to be done every rehearsal. Consistency is very important. If the department creates a "Virtual Callboard" on-line, you can avoid the copying process and post the notes at the end of the day for everyone. All department heads (Props, Costumes, etc.) the director and technical director will need this information.

Sound Effects and Cues

Stage managers are responsible for calling the start and stop of scenes. Do this by saying "Lights up" (down) or just "Lights." You will also need to approximate any sound effects. Be consistent with these verbal cues and sound effects during rehearsal. Note them in the prompt script and remember that actors will come to rely on what you give them.

Prompting

When an actor finds herself or himself unable to recall the lines, the stage manager must prompt them by feeding them their next line. The appropriate way for an actor to request a line is to simply say "Line" while remaining in character. You can either feed the actor the first couple of words, or give them the whole line.

Occasionally, long pauses are intentional so don't jump in. Feeding a line when it isn't necessary upsets actors and disrupts the scene. Having to search for the line and make everyone wait is also disruptive.

Keep your eyes in the book and be sensitive to the scene, pace and actors' patterns and behavior. When you prompt, be loud and clear.
When it comes to line corrections, every director prefers a different method. One might ask that you interrupt an actor every time they make a mistake. Another director might ask that you take note of the mistake and pass on the information later. Sometimes it depends on the mistake itself. You may end up interrupting when a line is jumped and take note when a line is jumbled or completely fabricated. Discuss with your director how she or he wants these problems handled. The same goes for blocking errors.

Timing

One of the stage manager's most important tools is a stop watch. You should time everything. Record the running time of every scene or act, scene shifts, etc. eventually, you will develop a target time for the production. Any major variations will indicate that there is a problem. Consistency is important.

Think about how long it takes to get from one side of the campus to the other, and in the rain. How long does it take to walk to your favorite sub shop and back to the theatre? What's the worst case parking scenario? How much is being wasted discussing the details of next week's makeup call? How long does it take for you to get the cast warmed up and focused? How long does it take to walk from backstage to the balcony through the inside of the building? Outside? You may not see the significance of these random bits of information now, but I guarantee you, at some point you will.

By now you should understand the importance of rehearsals. They are the true heart of the process, where the production takes shape. It is your responsibility to see that these rehearsals are run smoothly and efficiently as possible.

Vocal Warm-Ups

Big Black Bugs Bleed Blue Black Blood

Baby Bubble, Baby Bubble, Baby Bubble

Paper Poppy, Paper Poppy, Paper Poppy

Good Blood, Bad Blood

Girl Gargoyle, Guy Gargoyle

Red Leather, Yellow Leather

Unique New York, New York Unique

Toy Boat, Toy Boat, Toy Boat

Aluminum Linoleum Chrysanthemum Geranium

Which witch whined when the wine was spilled on the wailing whale?

A proper cup of coffee in a proper copper coffee cup

I slit the sheet, the sheet I slit, and on the slitted sheet I sit.

She sifted thistles through her thistle-sifter.

To sit in solemn silence on a dull dark dock in a pestilential prison with a life long lock, awaiting the sensation of a short sharp shock from a cheap and chippy chopper on a big black block.

Who washed Washington's white woolen underwear
when Washington's washwoman went west?

What a to do to die today a minute or two. A thing that's distinctly hard to say, but harder still to do.

A flea and a fly flew up in a flue.
Said the flea, "Let us fly!"
Said the fly, "Let us flee!"
So they flew through a flaw in the flue.

On mules we find two legs behind
and two legs before.
We stand behind before we find
what those behind be for.

Amidst the mists and coldest frosts,
with stoutest wrists and loudest boasts,
he thrusts his fist against the post
and still insists he sees the ghosts.

One-One was a racehorse.
Two-Two was one, too.
When One-One won one race,
Two-Two won one, too.

Physical Warm-Ups

There are a variety of exercises, games and other methods a director will use to get a cast prepared. Some directors may spend five minutes on warm-us and others may spend thirty minutes. The goal is to focus the actors physically and mentally.

Here are just a few options to get you started. As you work with different directors you will discover more.

Inhale/exhale - Several deep breaths, repeated at least 5 to 10 times. Remind actors to continue this same steady breathing while doing:
✔ Standard stretches
✔ Shoulder rotations
✔ Spine-rolls, begin by stretching chin to chest and slowly roll spine and reach toward toes, hold, reverse the process.

Make the "HUH" sound by pushing with the diaphragm, repeat several times

Jaw drop - stretch to the right and then left. Repeat several times.

Kiss and Smile - Stretch lips as far out as possible and pull back in.

Tongue stretch - Stick out tongue and stretch from left to right

Shakedown - Shake out the right arm eight times, then the left arm eight times, then the right leg eight times, then the left leg eight times. Then shake out all limbs seven times. This should be done fairly rapidly.

Reminders for Rehearsal

➢ Be early
➢ Clear the stage of anything that isn't used in the show.
➢ Clear backstage paths and wings.
➢ Sweep thoroughly.
➢ Set furniture and props. Spike as necessary.
➢ As actors arrive encourage them to begin with their own warm-up, studying lines or some means of focus.
➢ Let the director know when stage and actors are ready. As much as possible, relieve the director of the need to call people to the stage and getting them quiet. Take control.
➢ Be loud and clear when calling "lights" to start/end a scene as well as when giving cues (phone rings, etc.) and giving lines.
➢ Listen closely to the director.
➢ When taking blocking notes make certain that notation is clear and decipherable. If you use short hand provide a key in the prompt script.
➢ Let the director know when there are only 30 minutes of rehearsal left.
➢ Time everything.
➢ Keep non-cast members off the set furniture and away from the props. Try to have theatre clear of everyone except cast and crew. You need as little distraction as possible.
➢ Don't allow actors to give sound cues or line corrections.
➢ Rehearsal reports!
➢ Have fun. Be happy. Set an example for the cast.
➢ After rehearsal put away all props.

Beyond Rehearsal

Stage management is a twenty-four hour a day job. You don't really need to work around the clock, but there are things that need to be done outside the theatre and beyond rehearsal times. This includes helping with prop searches, looking in on the scene and costume shops and attending meetings.

Production Meetings

Production meetings vary with each theatre venue, as far as how many people attend and how frequently they occur. However, there are several factors that remain the same no matter where you are. The first is that the director, stage manager(s), technical director, and designers are all present.

The second factor is the goal. The goal of production meetings is to compare notes on progress in each area. During the meeting each person should get the opportunity to speak regarding his or her duties. Questions are addressed about scheduling, the various requirements of the production and anything else relevant to the process.

Typically, the stage manager leads the meeting. In the high school setting you may not have as much control over production meetings as you will later in your career. Speak to the director and any faculty involved in advance, and request the opportunity to take control.

Be prepared for these meetings. Have an agenda, a list of questions or issues that need to be addressed. See to it that each item is dealt with and that all members of the meeting have systematically covered everything they wanted discussed. Be careful not to waste time. If an issue cannot be addressed and dealt with in three minutes you should consider moving on to other topics. If there is time at the end of the meeting, go back to it. If not, try scheduling a meeting with those people the issue directly involves, to have a more focused discussion.

51

Don't forget to make note of all questions, solutions, and other issues discussed. You should type these notes and distribute or email them to those who attended the meeting.

Prop Assistance

The head of props is in charge of finding, making, or buying any props needed for the show. You should consider offering to help. Your props master may not need it, but he or she will be glad to know that you are willing to go thrift store shopping or digging through prop storage with them.

Shop visits

A lot of work takes place on a production outside of rehearsals. Don't be a stranger to it! Visit the shops when crews are working either after school or on Saturday workdays. You are probably expected to be there on Saturdays, but if not, go anyway, at least for a little while.

It is important that you are aware of the work involved in the building of the sets and costumes. Among other things you will understand the demands on your fellow company members and they will recognize your support for them and your commitment to the show. This will reinforce the team-work mentality as well as strengthen your relationships with technical crews.

Reflection

You have been absorbing a great deal of information in rehearsals that can't be entirely processed before you leave the theatre. No matter how busy your days are, there is always some time to think, even while washing your hair, or standing in line at the store, while taking a leisurely walk around campus, or waiting for class to begin.

Think about your cast. How do they react to one another? Are they happy? Were there any mistakes you made in rehearsal that you could make a conscious effort to avoid? What did you learn during the production meeting that will change the way you approach your job? Are there aspects of the set that you don't understand, like how the revolving stage works? The possibilities for discovery and preparation are endless. Don't turn your mind off of "stage manager mode" when you leave the theatre, or you may never make these discoveries.

Technical and Dress Rehearsals

Paper Tech

The stage manager, designers and director should meet to assign cues and other actions. Virtually every cue that will take place during a production gets noted in the script. The most common method is to assign a number to each light cue (1.0, 2.0 on up). Do the same for each sound cue, fly cue, etc. this point system will allow you to add cues as necessary through tech.

Some prefer to assign numbers to light cues and letters to sound cues. This is only beneficial if there are 26 or fewer sound cues. Once the letters start to double problems arise.

In the prompt script these cues should be noted in the margin of the script with a line clearly indicating its location. The letter "Q" is often used in place of the word "cue" in many situations. Applied in this case your notations would resemble LQ 2.0. Notations should be larger than the average writing size you have been using in the script. You don't want to be searching for them in a dimly lit booth during the show.

You should also prepare a master cue sheet noting the Cue#, the location, time span, description of effect and any other important information. For example, is it a visual cue and do any special things need to occur to make it happen?

Dry Tech

There are usually no actors called for what is known as "dry tech." The directors, designers and all technicians are present. This is an opportunity for the crew to learn their jobs, for the director to see light and sound effects, and for designers to make changes. This is also the time for the stage manager to see what the cues consist of and walk through scene shifts with the crew. Expect that cues will be added, deleted and moved around. Take concise notes on who is doing what to accomplish a cue.

Dry techs can be quiet and stress free. Be patient. Schedule a few breaks, bring some snacks and be in a good mood, to make certain that everything runs as smoothly as possible and that time isn't wasted. Let everyone know what the objectives are. Make certain that you understand everything that took place. If you still have questions when you leave the next technical run-thru, aka "tech," will suffer for it.

Tech

This will probably prove to be the longest and most difficult of all the days in the production process, however, it doesn't have to be a nightmare. With actors on stage you will move from Q to Q working out details. Just as technicians become familiar with how their jobs relate to the action of the play, the actors can become familiar with the technical efforts around them.

Depending on the script, the director's preferences and time constraints, most dialogue will probably be skipped to get to the next sequence of cues. On some occasions a scene or series of actions will need to be run through completely to set accurate timings to the cue changes. Actors need to remain in the house during tech so that they are ready as soon as they are needed. What is usually fifteen minutes worth of production time can last three minutes in tech and you don't want to be hunting for people all day. Some problems are simple and

can be noted and corrected later. For example, where a cue is called for the levels of light. Some problems are very large and need separate rehearsals; for example, complicated scene changes may need to be choreographed.

If a cue sequence does need to be repeated the stage manager should call "Hold" in a loud, firm voice, state the reason for the hold, have everyone restore to previous positions and cues. Give actors a line (a few lines before the sequence in question) put all operators on stand by and then give the actors the go.

Assistant stage managers should be seeing to the organization of props, assisting actors and taking notes on what goes on backstage, including scene shifts, props, etc.

Have glow tape ready. You can anticipate where most of the glow tape will have to be and can have it placed before tech (sides of wings, step units, furniture edges). It won't take long for an actor to discover places you have not considered. Don't go overboard with glow tape. When lights go black you don't want the audience to see a tiny universe of stars.

Expect actors to feel a little restless and uncomfortable in tech. They are used to being the center of attention. Make certain that you thank them for their patience. If they are being difficult, then let them know that you need for them to cooperate.

It will be a long day and/or night, have patience yourself, and stay focused. Many people will be expecting you to lead them through the process. Don't let them down. Others will be trying to do your job for you. Unless there is an emergency or a situation in which "faculty knows best," there is no reason for you to have to relinquish control.

Dress Tech

Dress tech is much the same as regular tech except that there are costumes and sometimes makeup. Hopefully, by this time all the kinks in the cues and scene shifts have been worked out. This rehearsal gives the director a chance to look at the costumes in relation to the overall design. It is not uncommon for the light designer to have to adjust light levels or colors to better coordinate with costumes. Also consider problems with the length and location of quick changes.

I would suggest that you again look over the set carefully, on stage and off, for any screws or nails that are sticking out of scenery or anything else that may pose a threat to both costumes and actors.

Dress Rehearsal

This is the full run of the show, all elements included. The stage manager should run it like a performance, stopping for serious problems only, especially safety issues. If a note can be taken and a problem fixed later then do not stop the run.

The Ultimate Scene Change

Ten to fifteen seconds. It sounds ridiculous, but ten seconds is actually a long time. Any longer and the audience will fall out of the illusion, or become uncomfortable, or bored. There are ways to borrow time but this requires either making the scene shift a part of the experience for the audience or perhaps using a distracting sound cue. So rehearse you scene changes. Use you crew to its full potential. Too many people in one change can create problems; people can help from the wings. Too few people involved can make for a long change. Choreograph changes to make them smooth and quick.

Anyone who goes on stage should be wearing black. They need to move with a purpose, but not rush. They should not look beyond the stage. They need to be aware of what others are doing during the shift so that they can compensate for anything overlooked. If the change is supposed to be in blackout, you may need to provide a little blue work light. It's always helpful to have someone off stage who can tell you when the change is complete and that the actors are in place.

Rehearsal Report Form

Production: _____

Director: _____

Date: _____ **Time:** _____

Stage Manager: _____

Cast present: _____

_____

_____

_____

Scene				
Run Time				

Breaks:

Props	Set
Lights	Sound
Costumes	Misc.

Performance

Everything a stage manager does on performance night is exciting. Performances are the test of your ability, and there is nothing better than rising to the challenge. Once you start the show its really time to sink or swim. Anyone can fill your space getting the show to curtain, but you are irreplaceable once the curtain is up. Ideally your prompt script would be good enough if it were necessary to have someone fill in, but you are the one who knows every inch of the show; the feel, the sound, the look. Each night, though actions and words are the same, the effect can be completely different. You are an integral part of that magic.

Have you ever had that feeling before a show, as a stage manager, or an actor, or a technician, that many like to call "stage fright?" Your palms get sweaty, your knees get weak, and your stomach has butterflies. Don't let it scare you away from anything. If you pay attention to your body you will notice that all your senses are becoming more acute - your hearing, your vision, etc. it means that you are battle ready. Use this feeling to find focus and the calm required to get the job done.

Focus everything on the show. Be prepared for anything. Doors mysteriously locking, leading to delayed or relocated entrances which will alter timing or visual cues. Something breaking on stage will force you to act fast to give your ASM an immediate solution, or warn your board ops of a change in plans. Some times there is absolutely nothing that can be done. You have to bite your knuckles and see what happens. Your awareness, judgement and problem solving skills will truly be called upon during a production. No matter what happens, always remember that to dwell on mistakes leads to more! Beat yourself up later, much later, if you must, though it's a waste of time.

You know by now the importance of being early, however, on production nights the stakes are higher and there are even more reasons to arrive early. Call for cast and crew should be at least one hour before the show. Give yourself enough time to be able to sit down in the theatre alone and get comfortable with the atmosphere, the silence, or lack of it; find the energy that exists there and let it seep into you. Clear your mind. Don't even worry about production, just breathe, listen and relax. This may sound unusual, but by doing it you ground yourself, your energy and focus within the theatre walls. Even if you only

59

have a couple of minutes before call, it is a good thing to do.

It is important that you have a routine and do things in the same order each night. You may not realize it but others may base their routine on yours. People will come to depend on seeing you in certain places at the same time every night. Just as they are getting to know what you are doing, you should be aware of what others are doing. It doesn't take too much to distract someone from her or his routine and lead them to overlook the obvious and even most critical of tasks.

Let's say that you are working your way around the building giving calls. For the first three performances, at this point in your rounds, you have always seen the same two techies outside the shop preparing the fog machine for Act.2. On the night of the fourth performance they aren't there. See this as a red flag. Changes in the routine can be a forecast of trouble ahead. Have someone find those two techies and confirm that the machine is ready.

Pre-Show

The most efficient way to handle pre-show duties is to have a check list. By following it closely you will minimize mistakes and second guessing on whether or not you did something. With any luck you will have an assistant stage manager to help you complete these tasks. You can use the following or create your own checklists.

stage photo

More than Half Hour Checklist:

- ☐ Sweep and/or mop the stage
- ☐ Turn on all equipment: circuit breakers, headsets, light board, monitors. (Crew can do some of these).
- ☐ Stage inspection (do this yourself). Walk through all doors & check windows. Any wet paint? Is all furniture on spike? Is everything functioning properly?
- ☐ See that all props are properly preset, on and off stage.
- ☐ Make certain that all practicals are working, anything powered on the set like lamps or radios.
- ☐ Check the wings for clutter, safety hazzards, etc.
- ☐ Witness light and sound checks.
- ☐ Make certain all cast members have arrived.
- ☐ Repeatedly check on the actors. When an actor needs you and you are nowhere to be found, they will get upset. Don't abandon them. Give them all the support you can.
- ☐ Make certain that the actors do good vocal and physical warm-ups.
- ☐ Make certain that everyone feels ok. You don't want a surprise illness during the performance.
- ☐ Allow everyone to check his or her props, etc.
- ☐ Supervise "fight call" on stage (run 2 or 3 times).
- ☐ Turn out work lights and do a blackout check.
- ☐ Start light and sound pre-shows
- ☐ Tell house manager when the stage is set and he or she can open the house.
- ☐ Call ½ hour at 33 -35 minutes to curtain time.
- ☐ Warn everyone that the house is open.

Less Than Half Hour Checklist:

☐ Meet with your crews. Give any notes, answer any questions. Let them now that you are counting on them and have confidence in them.

☐ Keep *everyone* out of the booth except your ops, including the director and technical director.

☐ Remind cast & crew of the need for silence and good behavior backstage.

☐ Call *fifteen minutes to places* at 20 minutes to curtain.

☐ Call *ten* at 15 minutes to curtain.

☐ Call *five* at 10 minutes to curtain.

☐ At 5 minutes to curtain, call a *stand by for places*.

☐ Check with house manager.

☐ Call *places*.

☐ Make final check with house manager.

☐ Check that crew is in position. Do roll call over the headset.

☐ Put everyone into *stand-by* and take a deep breath.

☐ Start the show on time. Don't hold the curtain.

Performance Checklist:

☐   Start the performance.

☐   Record start and stop times of each act and intermission. Crew should wait 2 minutes into intermission before change.

☐   Make *five minute* and *place* calls during intermission.

☐   Make certain all actors and crew are in their places.

☐   Put all on *stand-by*.

☐   Close the performance.

☐   Record total run time.

Post Show Checklist:

☐ Wait for house to clear before crew begins crossing the stage.

☐ Have your assistant stage manager and crews put everything in its place and ready for the next performance. Help as much as possible.

☐ All booth equipment off and locked up.

☐ Give any notes and announcements to cast and crew.

☐ Turn off lights.

☐ Lock theatre.

☐ Make certain that no one leaves alone.

Headsets and Calling Cues

✔ There should be no talking on headsets that is not in reference to cues or the status of the production. No gossip!

✔ Call cues clearly and quietly.

✔ Call stand-by's with plenty of warning. Take into account what the operator has to do before ready. Pushing one button will require less warning than manual board operation.

✔ Operators should acknowledge stand by, as example by stating, "lights standing by" so that the stage manager knows they are ready.

✔ If you are putting several operators on stand-by at once, wait for each one to acknowledge before moving on.

✔ Find the optimum place to start the call and mark it in the script. Anticipate - don't call a GO when the effect is to happen, but a second before. Execution of a cue takes time.

✔ If you get anxious before a cue, breath and focus. Cue anxiety can lead to jumping the gun or missing the cue completely.

The Booth

All booths are different. There are probably some that are brand new, with plenty of space and technology that lets you execute cues with the push of a single button. They might even have air conditioning, comfortable seats and working headsets with plenty of backup batteries. If this is the booth you are working in, then you are lucky.

Most booths are dark, crowded spaces that have cords draped this way and that. They have manual light boards and maybe three or four generations worth of different sound equipment. Find out what everything in the booth is before the production week if possible. You need to feel comfortable in the booth and the best way to do this is to know how things work, where they are plugged in, where the cords lead, and so on.

No matter what kind of booth you are in, there is always a button that shouldn't be touched. Usually, it's one on the light board. If one night you take the house lights out and the Pre-show out then call for lights up and nothing happens, it's probably because of the mystery button. Sometime after the house opened, it was accidently pushed. A new stage manager might panic until the board operator figures it out. A trained stage manager would turn instantly to the button, and a good stage manager would check the light board before taking out the house lights. The point is, you don't want any surprises, so be familiar with the booth.

Refining Your Performance

Each night you will discover better ways to do your job. Note things that happen too fast, or too late, or changes that were too long. Each night you will find more effective ways to relay information to the crew that will ultimately make things better.

Just as the actors need to feel an intimate connection to the production, so does the stage manager. When it comes to calling cues and running a performance it is critical that you feel the rhythm and the energy of the play. If they don't become a part of you then your cues will be ill timed and the play will be rocky.

Learn to anticipate. If, for example, a light should change when a door opens, call a cue just before the door opens. If a cue should happen on a specific word call it a beat before the word. But be warned, doors won't always open when you expect them to, and lines get rearranged. These things can make or break a performance and you have to feel it with everything in you. Distractions can be fatal.

Performance Reports

Performance reports are just as important to a production company as rehearsal reports are. They provide useful information to producers, house managers and everyone else involved. You should get into the habit of recording the necessary information every night.

Performance information should include the following:

1. Name of production, director, stage manager, date and location

2. Scheduled curtain time and actual curtain time

3. Run time of all acts and intermission & total for the show.

4. Audience: estimated number of audience members, any special guests, observations, audience response to the performance

5. Technical issues: anything that needs to be fixed, checked or re-spiked

6. Actor notes: missed lines, altered blocking, etc.

7. Anything out of the ordinary

Reminders for Performance

✎ Make certain that all equipment is turned on and warming up at least an hour before the show.

✎ Make certain all actors do good vocal and physical warm-ups.

✎ Make certain that light and sound checks are done well before the half-hour.

✎ Avoid unnecessary talk on headsets.

✎ Keep actors off headsets.

✎ Once the show has started, do not leave the booth! Backstage stage manager/assistant stage managers should try to stay in one place when you aren't dealing with props or changes. Actors will always know where to find you.

✎ Don't forget how much sound carries from backstage to the house, especially with no set. Keep things quiet backstage.

✎ Performance Reports - Date, Run, Timings, Problems, Comments, etc.

✎ After the show, find out if there were any problems that you weren't aware of.

✎ Check that all your props are put away.

✎ Make certain that all equipment is in the booth and backstage, and that the booth is locked up.

✎ Thank everyone for doing a good job.

Strike

What goes up must come down. After the closing night performance, cast and crew are always full of excitement and energy. There is a sense of relief and pride, and teamwork as well. The production may be over, but the process is not. The set must come down and the props and costumes need to be returned to their places. Don't forget to clean off the callboard and remove tape from the stage.

Strike can be many things. It can be long, exhaustive and even painful, both physically and emotionally. All students involved with the production should attend, including the stage manager. This part of the process can offer many people a sense of closure that doesn't take place the night before. As the stage manager, you are not required to have any authority or control during strike, however, you can use your people skills to keep everyone productive and in good spirits.

The Evaluation

It is important as a stage manager to evaluate your performance. You can start at any point in the process. In the form of an experience journal, record such things as issues with the director and their outcome, artistic choices that you agreed or disagreed with, and problematic situations in rehearsal and how you dealt with them. Write down your strengths and weaknesses.

Watch things critically, know why things work or don't work for a production. What do you think of the performance (costumes, lights, set, acting) and why? How does the audience reaction change from night to night? Include information about people, opinions, concerns, miracles, nightmares, funny stories, goals for the next rehearsal or next show that you stage manage. What are you proud of, or not proud of? What could you have done better? How have you changed since the process started? Be honest. The sooner you start in the process, the more you will see a change in your self and your job.

Preservation

For most people the show is over on closing night. Scripts go on the shelves and posters on the wall. As the stage manager you should consider a more historical outlook. The prompt script should carry nearly every detail about the production. In theory it should be able to be reproduced years down the road. Take photographs of rehearsals, the set being built, the props that are used, anything and everything. Keep ground plans. Make a video.

NOTES

Part 3:
Useful Information

Potential Course Plan for Teachers:

(Discussion points and quizzes on pages 77 through 80 are included for your convenience.)

The Art of Stage Management

Discussion: **The ten skills and qualities of a stage manager**

Assignment: **Awareness**
Take class into the theatre. Have them look around. Prepare a list of questions based on that visit. What potential safety hazards did you notice? Were there tools on stage or in the wings? Did it appear that someone had recently been there?

Assignment: **Journal Entry**
Outside of class incorporate what you learn about motivation and respect while interacting with others. Try to motivate someone. Document an event in which you put to use one or more if these skills.

Quiz 1: See page 77
Name the 10 skills and qualities of a stage manager and give at least three reasons they are important to the job, or other relevant factors.

Discussion: **Safety** – Take your own theatre conditions into account.

Quiz 2: Safety see page 77

The Process of Stage Management

<u>Discussion</u>: **Relationships and the Role of a stage manager**

<u>Assignment 1</u>: **Prompt book**
Each student chooses a script, takes appropriate dividers etc., script layout etc. and scene breakdowns.

<u>Assignment 2</u>: **Script research**
Create requirement lists for each category: Lights, Sound, Props, Costumes, SFX

<u>Discussion:</u> **Production in Progress**

<u>Assignment 3</u>: **Rehearsal observations**
Each student should attend at least 3 rehearsals of the current production at the school, then document that experience.

<u>Assignment 4</u>: **Warm-ups and games**
Have each student submit different games and warm ups that they know or have created on their own and eventually you can create a class compilation.

<u>Assignment 5</u>: **Blocking, long & short**

<u>Assignment 6</u>: **Reports**
Create rehearsal report form template for chosen script

<u>Quiz 1</u>: Rehearsal quiz: See page 78

<u>Discussion:</u> **Tech: Transition into Performance**

<u>Assignment 7</u>: **Production and Technical information**
Create performance report form template and create tech information: preset list, crew assembly, and backstage plans.

Quiz 2: Tech Quiz: See page 78

Discussion: **Performance**

Assignment 8: **Attend a current production and review it in detail**

Quiz 3: Performance Quiz: See page 79

Discussion: **Meet with the SM('s) of a current production**

Final: **Prompt Book and Journal**
Turn in book with blocking key, partially blocked script, mock sheets, etc.

Discussion Points or Quizzes

Stage Management: Skills and Qualities

List 10 skills and qualities required for stage management, and give at least one reason why each is important.

1. _____
2. _____
3. _____
4. _____
5. _____
6. _____
7. _____
8. _____
9. _____
10. _____

Stage Management: Safety

Name at least four safety precautions from the check list in the book and come up with at least one that applies to your school's theatre.

1. _____
2. _____
3. _____
4. _____
5. _____

Stage Management: Rehearsal
Name four things that should be said or done at the start of your first rehearsal.

1. _____
2. _____
3._____
4.

_____

Name 4 things that should be included in your set-up routine.

1. _____
2. _____
3. _____
4. _____

What is spiking, and how is it done?

_____
_____
_____
_____
_____
_____
_____
_____

Stage Management: Tech
Who is involved in a Paper Tech?
_____
_____
_____
_____
_____

What is the purpose of a Dry Tech?

_____
_____
_____
_____

What is the difference between a Dress Tech and a Dress Rehearsal?

_____
_____
_____
_____

What information about cues is included on a master cue sheet?

_____
_____
_____
_____

Stage Management: Performance
List 10 pre-show duties

1. _____
2. _____
3. _____
4. _____
5. _____
6. _____
7. _____
8. _____
9. _____
10. _____

Think of 4 "what ifs" and possible solutions to each.

1. _____
2. _____
3. _____
4. _____

What 3 skills will help most when calling a show?

1. _____
2. _____
3. _____
4. _____

Name 5 things that should be included in a performance report?

1. _____
2. _____
3. _____
4. _____
5. _____

Examples of Typical Forms
Used in Stage Management

THE GRANNY (LA NONA)
ACTOR/ SCENE BREAK DOWN

	NONA	CARMELO	CHICHO	MARIA	ANYULA	MARTA	FRANSICO
1-1 1-22	X	X	X	X	X	X X	
1-2 23-31	X	X	X	X X	X		
1-3 32-33	X X	X	X	X			
1-4 34-38		X	X	X		X X	
1-5 35-46			X				X
1-6 47-58	X	X	X	X	X	X	X
2-1 59-60	X						X
2-2 61-70	X	X	X	X	X	X	X X
2-3 71-77	X X	X	X	X	X		X X
2-4 78-85	X .	X	X	X	X	X	
2-5 86-89	X	X	X	X	X X	X	
2-6 90-92	X	X	X	X			
2-7 93-95	X		X	X			

Private Eyes

Requirements Lists : **Sound**

Page	Music		Artist	In	Out
Act One					
p. 63	Is You Is Or Is You Ain't My Baby	(Intro)	Joe Jackson	Black	End of intro
p. 68	Is You Is Or Is You Ain't My Baby	(instrumental)		>"lunchtime	Fades w/ Lisa at table
p. 71	I Want You		Tom Waits	Lisa's exit	Snaps >"Lets take 5"
p. 80	Is You Is Or Is You Ain't My Baby	(final c. to end)		>"Lets eat"	Song ends
p. 90	Tell the Truth		Ray Charles	M. snaps	Lights shift
p. 91	Can I Steal a Little Love		Frank Sinatra	>B.O	
Act Two					
p. 92	Fever		Peggy Lee	Black	Snaps w/ Lights up
p. 102	Don't Explain		Dexter Gordon	with Kiss	Fades > "I see that"
p. 106	Please Be Kind		Ella Fitzgerald	Light shift	Fades by "Ad. Ross"
p. 107	Am I Wrong? (First verse)		Keb Mo	>"what then?"	Matthews entrance
p. 109	Moon Love		Chet Baker	Cory vanishes	Lights up on Studio
p. 118	Eerie music				
p. 122	Gun shot (echoes)			>"Goodbye"	
p. 124	I Want You		Tom Waits	M. snaps fingers	song concludes

Private Eyes
Rehearsal Report Form

Director: Robin Armstrong
Stage Manager: Eliza Ward

Date: 8/14/01
Time: 7-9:45

Cast present:
    Kristen, Jack, Sunny, Peter

Scenes	1: 5	1: 6	1: 7	p. 80-91
Run Time	5:10	6:20	7:03	16:33

BREAKS: 8-8:06   8:56 –9:01

Props	Set – Robin wants to keep small lamp on concession stand
Sc.5 – 3 wine glasses w/wine, 3 forks + knives, pad of paper, wait tray, pencil; 3 party hats +party favors; 3 cameras Sc. 6- 3 salads, 3 dressings, 1 fork, napkin; vile of poison. Sc. 7- peppermill	She also wants tall floor lamp for USL corner (hotel room) What do you think?
Lights Sc.5 Restaurant: R of DSR (Floor) Sc.6 Wait Stand: bottom of stairs and concession area Sc. 7 Restaurant- (death scene)	**Sound**
Costumes 3 Trench coats – Polly, Betzi, Frank	**Misc.** Ask **Steph**. About waitstaff stuff Call **Amanda** again **All contracts and bios due Mon. 20th 5:30 PM

mate can	on shelf by stove
kettle	on stove
newpaper	Chichos room
rolls	6 in basket
ledger	in rt. drawer in Green
soup bowls	in cupboard
plates	in cupboard
wine glasses	13 in bar
wine	at bar
13 forks,spoons,knives	at bar
corkscrew	in left drawer of Green
stew pot	on stove
soup pot	on stove
2 ladles	at stove
fruit basket with 4 apples and 1 banana	on fridge
rag	at sink
grappa	on bar
shot glasses	on bar
frying pan	on green thing by stove
knife	on Green
shopping cart and bag	in closet
potato chips	in Green
Marias coin purse w $	on dR table
phone	on dR table
water pitcher	in cupboard
martas purse	under dR table
bell	in chichos room
bottle of pills	above sink
water glasses	in cupboard
pistol	in chichos room
pickel relish	fridge
sandwhich makings	fridge
parmesean	fridge
2 yellow cheeses	fridge
dish soap	above sink
cleaning liquid	above sink
3 jars	above sink
ornaments	shelf above clipboard
ornaments	shelf above fridege
olive oil/vinegar/olive oil	shelf by stove
salt and pepper	shelf by stove
salad bowl w/ fork	green next to stove
turn on burner	
dish holders	at sink
munchies	fridge
plate of rolls	fridge
eggs	fridge
extra jars	fridge

MASTER CUE SHEET

PRODUCTION: GLENGARRY GLEN ROSS

Cue #	Pg #	Effect	Cue Word + Track	Level	Speed
L 1 + S1	7	PRESET/PRESHOW ♪			
L 1.5 + S 2	7	H ½ + PRESHOW ♪ ↓			
S 3	7	1.1 INTRO	TRACK 10	M 4	
L 2	7	H ↓ + PRESET ↓			
L 3 + S 4	7	L ↑ (sc. 1) + S ↓	W. TAPS ON BOWL		
L 4 + S 5	15	B.0 + S ↑ + shift lights	"Hotel" TRACK 11	M 5	
L 5 + S 6	15	L ↑ (sc. 2) + S ↓	LISTEN FOR IT		
L 6 + S 7	27	B.0 + S ↑ + shift lights	"Because you listened" TRACK 12	M 5	
L 7 + S 8	27	L ↑ (sc. 3) + S ↓	GLOW OF CIG. AND SILENCE ON STAGE		
L 8 + S9	30	B.O + S ↑	"Listen...gonna tell you" TRACK 13	M 6	
L 9 + S 10	30	PRESET AND INT. ♪	TRACK 14	M 6	
L 9.5	31	H ½			
L 10 + S 11	31	H ↓ + PRESET ↓	TRACK 21	M 5	
L 11 + S 12	31	L ↑ + INT. ♪ ↓			
L 12 + S 13	65	B.0 + CURTAIN ♪	"I'll be at the restaurant" TRACK 23	FADE ↑ to 7 +	
L 13	65	CURTAIN CALL L ↑			
L 14	65	B.O			
L 15 + S 16	65	PRESET, H, MARCH ↑			

*WORK LIGHTS AND BS LAMP ON POWER STRIP NEAR BACK STAIRS

Pre-show
6:30 – 7:30
- Turn on sound equipment – three power ups – (amp. Under table and both table top units)
- Sound check
- Dimmer check- (Nikki will do when she comes in)
- Sweep
- Set stage for top of show – check spikes – (see preset sheet)
- Check in on actors
- Have actors check props and walk stage
- Prep lo mein and set sl
- Make drinks for 1.2+3
- Preset lights and pre show music ↑

7:30-8:00
- Call ½ hour
- Check with HM – Open House
- Turn heat off
- Call 15 at 7:43 meet with crew
- Call 10 – at 7:48
- Call 5 at 7 – check with House
- Call places 2 min. before 8:00

**** EXTRAS ARE IN BOX ON PROPS TABLE IN GREEN ROOM – LIKE COOKIES. CHOPSTIX. LEADS ETC.****

PRESET COSTUMES:

1.1
W's. CASE –C. LEFT BENCH SIDE
L's. JACKET – FAR LEFT BENCH SIDE
Aa.'s – RAIN COAT ON COAT RACK UP STAGE

Intermission

2.1
M. JACKET- SL ROLLING CHAIR (d.l. usually places it after his scene Act 1.)
Aa. JACKET – ON COAT RACK (chris leaves on desk during Act.1)

PRESET TOP OF SHOW:

ALL UPSTAGE FURNITURE FOR ACT 2 IN PLACE
- TABLE W/ BROCHURES AND MAGAZINES IN WAITING AREA (UC)
- CHAIR UC
- TWO FILE CABINETS ON SPIKE
- COAT RACK ON SPIKE – SR   Aa. OVER COAT ON COAT RACK
- TABLE WITH MAIL BOX – SL
- WATER COOLER – SL

OFF SPIKE BEHIND SCREEN   TRAY W/ ROCKS GLASS ON SR DESK (½ GINGERALE)
- 2 ROLLING / 2 NON ROLLING CHAIRS   GIMLET SR (MOUNTAIN DEW)
- 2 DESKS   HIGHBALL (COKE) ON BLACK FILE CABINET
- BLACK FILE CABINET

FOLDING SCREENS

2 BOOTHS ON SPIKE   W.'S CASE C.LEFT BENCH SIDE
2 RED CUSHION CHAIRS   L'S .JACKET FARLEFT BENCH SIDE
2 TABLES

SC. 1 PRESET – CONDIMENTS AND ASHTRAY ON BOTH TABLES
(SL TABLE)
- LO MEIN IN BOWL
- CHOPSTIX + XTRA IN PACK
- 2 RED NAPKINS
- 2 TEA CUPS WITH H20
- 2 CHECKS
- TEAPOT W/ H20

SHIFT 1

SET – 2 GLASSES, CHECK, COOKIES, 2 NAPKINS
STRIKE – ALL SL. TABLE CONTENTS EXEPT CONDIMENTS AND ASHTRAY
        SL. CHAIR

SHIFT 2

STRIKE – CHAIR SR
SET –   BOOTHS TOGETHER, TABLES MOVED A LITTLE
STRIKE – SR TABLE CONTENTS

INTERMISSION   MAKE SURE NIKKI DOES REPATCH *

STRIKE THROUGH OFFICE DOOR   (CREW WILL DO THIS)
STRIKE SCREEN
STRIKE TABLE STUFF
STRIKE TABLES
STRIKE BOOTHS
                        (CREW HELPS)
SET FILE CABINET TO DSL – OPEN 2^(ND) DRAWER ONLY A FEW INCHES FOR THE STUFF TO POKE OUT
SET DESKS ON SPIKE
SET 2 ROLLING CHAIRS AND OTHER TWO CHAIRS - (SL NON ROLL CH. ON SIDE)
SET CHICAGO TRIBUNE ON SL ROLLING CHAIR
SET ASHTRAY EACH DESK   BOARD GOES UP
SET BRIEFCASE SL DESK ON FLOOR
TOSS PAPERS ETC. – SOME CENTER, AND ALSO AROUND FILE CABINETS
SET PAPERS AND NOTEPAD ON SL DESK
SET PLEXI SHARDS
SOME DRAWERS OPEN............

END OF NIGHT

PICK UP LOOSE PAPERS AND FILES → DESK BINS
PLAYBOY → DRAWER (2ND DOWN)
DESKS → CENTER
PLEXI → BOX
2 ROLL CHAIRS → US
2 NON ROLL → UC
BOARD → SAFE PLACES UC

MARLBORO BOX → JUSTIN SPOT IN GREEN ROOM
LEVENENS JACKET (LEFT BACK STAGE) → TO GREEN ROOM
THROW AWAY USED CHOPSTIX
ALL OTHER PROPS BACK TO GREEN ROOM
WASH OUT USED DISHES
PRESETS OUT
WORK LIGHTS OUT WHEN READY TO GO (SWITCH IS ATTACHED LEG OF TABLE IN BOOTH
LIGHT BOARD STAYS ON WITH MASTER ↓   A+ B ↓
ALL THREE SOUND THINGS OFF

GLENGARRY GLEN ROSS

Production Meeting Notes
2/10/02
6 pm Firehouse

Attendance: Morrie, Tom, Liz, Paige, David, Carol, Pam

NEXT MEETING: Saturday Feb. 16th   6 PM

TOM
-Dominion sponsoring opening night reception
-Picking up poster and post card proofs this week at Printers Mark
-Should have banner this week

CAROL
-Everything is on schedule
-Interview with WCVE will air on Feb.24
-Needs comps for John
-STYLE will be here for open
-64 Magazine is going to do an article – Dave Timerbline – needs comps
-Roy Proctor will be at open

DAVID
-Productive weekend. – some walls up, platforms in, lights hung....
-Things are on schedule – lights a little ahead
-Work lights now on separate switch – in booth
-Had no volunteers today
-Stage useable from now on
-Banquettes redesigned
-Needs to see the screen from Marthas Mixtures
-4 x 8 Hollywood flats upstairs could be another option

PROPS
-Need one metal desk
-D.asks all to consider where to locate water cooler – old – brown base with blue jug
-cut from list- ashtrays, register area items

WORK CALL – **Saturday 9 am & Sunday 10 am**
-need 4 people to work in theatre on set
-need additional 4 to load/unload desks
-Tom arranging truck for desk move

MISC
-DOUG JOHNSON – needs to be added as ASSISTANT TECHNICAL DIRECTOR
-Pam has made contacts with HANOVER JUVENILE CENTER – increased volunteer pool
-Will need run crew starting February 24th
-Need to know how many people expected to be used for running crew – Doug, any idea?

SCHEDULE
Saturday, Feb. 16th @ 6 PM – PR. MTNG – NOT SUNDAY
Sunday, Feb. 17th @ 7 PM – Paper tech
Monday, Feb. 18th @ 7 PM – Dry Tech – poss. Q-Q w/actors
Tuesday, Feb. 19th @ 7 PM - work thru
Wednesday, Feb. 20th @ Full run with costume 7:00 call, 8:00 GO – and photos

Private Eyes   Production Meeting Notes 8-24

Monday Aug. 27th

Run thru scheduled for Tuesday, August 28, 2001 – for designers to see changes

Hotel curtain may need to be two separate curtains – depends on traveler that can be fashioned

All drapes SR need to be removed

David and Steph will meet soon to pick up bed from the Dray's

Stephanie working on getting the peppermill, plate cover and ramicans

Chairs – spray paint metal chairs and re-cushion

Tablecloth to be burgundy – Stephanie has fabric

Green door backstage will be covered

Posters, Flyers etc. are being printed

Pictures come in tomorrow

Next meeting: 5:30 Tuesday, August 4th

91

Sound Cues

Production: _Thunder_

SM: E. Ward
Date: Feb. 10
Page: 1 of 3

Cue No.	Page	Description	Cue Word	Length	Level	Speed
S 1	p.6	Thunder	(ent prologue)			
2	p.8	Thunder	tale...			
B1	p.12	Believe me	toes...			
B2	p.24	Big Money	mind...			
S3	p.34	Thunder	...Jaguar...			
+	p.36	Thunder	(Brandi kiss)	"Wait"		
∴						
5	p.40	Tension builder	Arm up B4 point			
		(Cuts off w/ A.S. stepping in)				
6	p.4	More drums	..hurt you..			
		(cutsoff w/A.S. stepping in)				
B3	p.47	Hurt Somebody	(G+G.S. exit)			
S7	p.47	Drum Loop	(J.+D. run for I)			
8	p.48	Thunder	(end of song)			
B4	p.50	See Through me	take a chance--			
S9	p.51	Thunder	Kiss			
10	p.51	Intermission	in Blackout			
S11	p.52	40 sec. loop	(with lights)			
12	p.56	dusting music	(visual-Drag)	w/ cork-ou		
13	p.57	Horn	(we home free)			
B5	p.61	Im Back	(w/ lights)			
B6	p.63	What Should I do	(after Momma)			
B7	p.64	Born w/ Blues	(with lights)			
S14	p.71	Moonsnake Dance	(Finger to Tongue)			
			Stops on S14			

Blank Forms to copy and use

Audition Form

\# _____

Production _____

Name _____ Class _____

Address _____

Phone \# _____ E-Mail _____

Special Skills:

_____

Potential Conflicts: (school, family, church, league sports, scouts etc.)

_____

_____

Be thorough – Once schedule is set you will be expected to attend.

Schedule - mark off the times you are in class or working. Be very clear. Rehearsals will be scheduled according to these forms. Some may be planned for the mornings, afternoons and evenings.

	Mon.	Tues.	Wed.	Thurs.	Fri.	Sat.	Sun.
8:00							
9:00							
10:00							
11:00							
12:00							
1:00							
2:00							
3:00							
4:00							
5:00							
6:00							
7:00							
8:00							
9:00							
10:00							

Rehearsal Report Form

Production: _____

Director: _____

Date: _____ **Time:** _____

Stage Manager: _____

Cast present: _____

_____

_____

_____

Scene				
Run Time				

Breaks:

Props	Set
Lights	**Sound**
Costumes	**Misc.**

PROP REQUIREMENTS

PRODUCTION:
DIRECTOR:
STAGE MANAGER: PG. ____ OF _____

ACT	SC.	PG	CHARACTER	USE	TRACKING NOTES

SOUND REQUIREMENTS

PRODUCTION:
DIRECTOR:
STAGE MANAGER: PG. _____ OF _____

ACT	SC.	PG	EFFECT	NOTES

LIGHT REQUIREMENTS

PRODUCTION:
DIRECTOR:
STAGE MANAGER: PG. _____ OF _____

ACT	SC.	PG	EFFECT	NOTES

SCENERY REQUIREMENTS

PRODUCTION:
DIRECTOR:
STAGE MANAGER: PG. ____ OF ____

ACT	SC.	PG	SCENIC ELEMENT	POSITION	NOTES

COSTUME REQUIREMENTS

PRODUCTION:
DIRECTOR:
STAGE MANAGER: PG. _____ OF _____

ACT	SC.	PG	CHARACTER	COSTUME	NOTES

SOUND CUE SHEET

PRODUCTION:
DIRECTOR:
STAGE MANAGER: PG. _____ OF _____

CUE #	PG #	EFFECT	CUE WORD OR ACTION	LEVEL	SPEED

LIGHT CUE SHEET

PRODUCTION:
DIRECTOR:
STAGE MANAGER: PG. _____ OF _____

CUE #	PG #	EFFECT	CUE WORD OR ACTION	LEVEL	SPEED

MASTER CUE SHEET

PRODUCTION:
DIRECTOR:
STAGE MANAGER: PG. _____ OF _____

CUE #	PG #	EFFECT	CUE WORD OR ACTION	LEVEL	SPEED
CUE #	PG #	EFFECT	CUE WORD OR ACTION	LEVEL	SPEED

Glossary

Acting area - The space in which the acting takes place.

Blackout - Absence of light on stage.

Breakaway - Prop or furniture item that is specifically designed to break.

Center state - Middle of the playing area.

Contact sheet - Contact information for everyone involved in the production.

Cross - An actor's movement from one area to another.

Down stage - Playing area at the front of the stage, nearest the audience.

Dry tech - Technical rehearsal without actors.

Flies - The area above the stage where scenery is hung.

Fly - Raising or lowering of scenery that hangs from flies.

French scene - A scene designated by an entrance and exit.

Gaffa Tape - Sticky cloth tape with multiple uses. Generally black in color.

Ghost light - A light left on after rehearsal or performance when the theatre is locked up.

Glow tape- Luminous tape strategically placed so actors can navigate in blackout.

Ground plan - A layout of the set drawn to scale.

Hand props - Props handled by the performers.

House - The audience area of the theatre.

Paper tech - Meeting between the stage manager, directors and designers during which all technical elements are recorded and cues assigned.

Personal props - Props that are specific to a character and are the responsibilty of the actor during the performance.

Places - A call for actors to take positions for ther start of the performance.

Practicals - Lights, props or other scenery elements that are not simply decorations, but can be used. Ex. Lights, radios.

Preset - To have props, costumes or other sets in place before the show begins.

Preset list - Details exactly what goes where.

Prompt script - A book kept by the stage manager that holds all information required for the production, including every stage direction, every light que and all thechnical requirements.

Read thru - Reading of the script by company. Generally done in the first rehearsal.

Requirement lists - List effects, props or costumes that are called for in the script.

Revolve - Rotating platform.

Run thru - Rehearsal of show from start to finish with no stops.

Shift - The changing of set between scenes.

Sides - Audition materials. Excerpts from script or other text that the director chooses.

Spike - A mark designating the place of a piece of furniture or set piece.

Stage directions - Notes detailing actions, blocking or other stage business.

Stage left - The left side of the stage if facing the audience.

Stage manager - Person responsible for coordinating all aspects of production, overseeing all rehearsals and orchestrating performances.

Stage right - To remove items during scene changes; the dismantling and removal of set, props, light equipment, etc. at the end of the run.

Up stage - Back of the stage.

Work lights - Soft glow of lights provided for stage crew to maneuver during scene shifts. Blue lights placed in backstage area where necessary.

Resources for Further Study

Stage Managing and Theatre Etiquette: A Basic Guide by Linda Apperson

The Stage Management Handbook by Daniel A. Ionazzi

The Back Stage Guide to Stage Management by Thomas A. Kelly

The Art and Craft of Stage Management by Doris Schneider

Stage Management by Lawrence Stern

Notes: